Marie Curie

Marie Curie

A SCIENTIFIC PIONEER

ALLISON LASSIEUR

FRANKLIN WATTS
A Division of Scholastic Inc.
New York Toronto London Auckland Sydney
Mexico City New Delhi Hong Kong
Danbury, Connecticut

Photographs © 2003: ACJC–Curie and Joliot Curie Archives: 8, 9, 12, 16, 21, 23, 26, 34, 37, 40 left, 43, 45, 46, 54, 61, 6
2, 73, 79, 92, 94; AIP Niels Bohr Library: 67; Brown Brothers: cover left, 40 right, 95; Corbis Images: 6, 70 (Bettman),
28 (Alexander Burkatowski), 30 (John Heseltine), 32 (Robert Holmes), 10 (Hulton-Deutsch Collection);
Getty Images/Roger Viollet: back cover, cover right, 56, 81; Hulton | Archive/Getty Images: 2, 58; Jay M. Pasachoff: 90;
Photo Researchers, NY: 64 (J-L Charmet/SPL), 97 (SPL); Science Museum/Science & Society Picture Library: 52, 82,
99; Stock Montage, Inc.: 48, 96.

Lassieur, Allison
  Marie Curie: a scientific pioneer / by Allison Lassieur
    p. cm. — (Great life stories)
Includes bibliographical references and index.
Contents: Early years in Poland—Launching a dream—A student in Paris—A new life—The great discovery—The
Nobel Prize, fame, and strange ailments—The dark years—New successes, new ordeals—World War I and the later
years—Timeline.
ISBN 0-531-12270-0
1. Curie, Marie, 1867–1934—Juvenile literature. 2. Chemists—Poland—Biography—Juvenile literature. [1. Curie, Marie,
1867–1934. 2. Chemists. 3. Scientists. 4. Women—Biography.] I. Title. II. Series.
  QD22.C8L37 2003
  540'.92—dc21

                                                                                            200300953

j Biography
Curie

Contents

This is how the Plac Krola Zygmunta III, a large Warsaw boulevard, probably looked when Manya lived there. During Manya's childhood Russian troops often gathered in areas like this around the city.

ONE

Early Years in Poland

Early November in Warsaw, Poland, was a cold and dreary time. Chill winds whipped the gray and brown buildings. Men and women filled the narrow streets, and the rattle of hundreds of carts echoed between the buildings. The day of November 7, 1867, was like any other winter day in the city.

One building, a girls' school, hummed with activity. Their teacher, Bronislawa Sklodowski, began the students' lessons. Soon, however, sharp pains in her abdomen signaled that her fifth child was about to be born. That evening a daughter came into the world, much to the delight of the students and of Bronislawa's other four young children: Zofia, Jozef, Bronya, and Helena. The baby's joyful mother named her Maria Salomea. The family nicknamed her Manya.

Manya's beloved mother, Bronislawa, was dedicated to her children. When Manya was very small, the family began taking in boarders to make money. It is believed that one of these boarders infected Bronislawa with the tuberculosis that eventually killed her.

A CHILD OF DEDICATED TEACHERS

Bronislawa and Vladyslaw Sklodowski, Manya's father, were honest, hardworking teachers who valued learning above everything. Bronislawa had been educated in Warsaw, at the prestigious Freta Street girls' school. In 1860, the year she married Vladyslaw, she became the headmistress of the school. As headmistress, she was given an apartment adjacent to the stately school, where the family lived.

Manya's father was also a very respected teacher. He was the director of a state-run high school called a gymnasium. He had a passion for learning and for teaching. Science was his favorite subject. Manya's father kept up with the newest scientific discoveries and even wrote articles about them that appeared in local publications. Vladyslaw's joy of learning and of the natural world strongly influenced all of his children, who came to love science and learning as much as he did.

Although Manya's family had a comfortable life, the situation outside its safe walls was a different matter. When Manya was born, the political condition in Poland was very bad for most of its citizens. They lived under the rule of the Russians, who had invaded the country many years before. In spite of this, Bronislawa and Vladyslaw were part of a generation that was fiercely proud of its Polish heritage.

POLAND'S DARK HISTORY

The Russian government treated Polish citizens harshly. As a result, the people harbored bitterness and anger that had been simmering for decades.

Twice before Manya was born, loyal Polish citizens had tried to fight their Russian oppressors. The first, called the November Uprising, occurred in 1830. The Russians defeated the Poles, and thousands of Polish people were imprisoned or exiled. The second great attempt of the Polish people to retake their country from the Russians took place during the winter of 1863. It was called the January Uprising. When the Polish were defeated this second time, the Russian government was especially harsh. Thousands of Poles were sent to

Vladyslaw, Manya's father, was convinced that education was the key to liberating Poland from Russian oppression. He taught all of his children to love Poland. Manya's fierce, lifelong patriotism came from her father's passion for their country and its culture.

Siberia, never to be seen again. Thousands more fled to other countries such as France. Poland was once again under harsh Russian rule.

For the next fifty years, throughout almost all of Manya's lifetime, the Russian government worked in Poland to erase all traces of Polish history, culture, and language. They replaced it with the Russian language and history. This "Russification" of Poland was designed to weed out every trace of Polishness in every citizen, for all time.

Polish people were routinely discriminated against. Russians got the highest-paying jobs. As one Danish visitor to Poland wrote, "If [a Polish citizen] studies law, he can never become a judge, generally not even an official. . . . If he studies medicine, he can never obtain a post [job] at a university, never be at the head of a hospital, never conduct a public clinic, therefore can never attain the first rank in his science."

Manya's father was a victim of this discrimination. When Manya was a small child, Vladyslaw was fired from his position of director of the gymnasium. Many people believed it was because he had angered his Russian

Russian troops gathered in Warsaw after the January Uprising. The January Uprising was a desperate attempt by the Polish people to throw off the Russian government. When the Polish were defeated, their hope of political freedom was gone.

A Call to Arms

When Manya's father, Vladyslaw, was a young man, he wrote a poem that described the oppression the Polish people felt under Russian rule. It ended with this plea for Poland to break free from the Russian tyrants:

> *Let us break this armor of ice that binds our chests*
> *Let us begin today, bring stones to build*
> *The temple of truth, the temple of freedom.*
> *Let our willpower cure our crippled souls*
> *Let our hard work prove—to the world,*
> *to God, to our country—our worth . . . "To the future!"*

superiors at the school. Although he eventually found another teaching position at a different gymnasium, he never lost his bitterness and anger at the Russians for the loss of his job.

DESPITE OPPRESSION, MANYA THRIVES ON LEARNING

The Russian oppression ignited a fierce sense of patriotism and loyalty in the hearts of all Polish people. The more that the Russian government cracked down, the more the Poles fought back. Many educated Poles understood that education was their only hope. Education could keep Polish history, language, and learning alive. Bronislawa and Vladyslaw set about to teach their children as much as they could, away from the oppressive eye of the Russians. They encouraged all of their children, including little Manya, to love learning.

Science and history were especially important to the Sklodowski family. Manya's father found lessons in even the most ordinary daily activities. If the family saw a beautiful sunset, for example, Vladyslaw used it to

Manya was the youngest child in the brilliant Sklodowski family. From left: Zofia, Helena, Manya, Jozef, and Bronya. Zofia died of typhus after this photograph was taken. Jozef and Bronya grew up to become respected physicians. Helena became an educator.

explain how sunsets happened. All of the Sklodowski children learned languages, including Russian, Polish, and English. At home, he even used equipment from the gymnasium where he worked to teach Manya and her siblings biology.

Vladyslaw made up games and activities for his children that were educational but also great fun. As a history lesson, he asked the children to make a collage of pictures from magazines and newspapers. Manya, Helena, and the other children loved to flip through magazines to find pictures for their collage. They had a set of colorful blocks that their father used for geography lessons. The blocks represented countries, rivers, cities, continents, and mountains. These lessons were often filled with noise and laughter as Vladyslaw and the children used the blocks to travel the world.

It became clear that Manya was especially intelligent. One day, when Manya was very small, she was watching her older sister Bronya struggle with a reading lesson. Suddenly Manya read the sentence aloud easily. Everyone stared at Manya in shock because she had not been taught to read yet. Manya, thinking she had done something terribly wrong, burst into tears and said, "I didn't know I wasn't supposed to do that, but it was so easy!"

The weekends were special for Manya and her brother and sisters. Every Saturday night from seven o'clock to nine o'clock their father read aloud to them, usually from Polish books that had been forbidden by the Russian government. Poetry was very important in the Polish culture at the time. Poets were seen as leaders, people who represented the feelings of the Polish people through their works.

Manya especially was affected by the power and emotion of the poetry her father read on these Saturday nights. Her lifelong love of poetry, especially from Polish poets, grew out of these readings. Later in life she was to say that those "evenings were for us a great pleasure and a source of renewed patriotic feelings."

CATASTROPHE IN MANYA'S LIFE

Manya's early years were filled with happiness and the comfort of a loving family. That was all to change when Manya was ten years old. That year her mother, Bronislawa, died of tuberculosis.

Bronislawa had been a strong, intelligent woman who loved her family and her work. At a time when few women held jobs with responsibility, Bronislawa was a respected headmistress of one of the best girls' schools in Poland. Between her work at the school and running a busy household, Bronislawa found little time to devote to each child. But she showed her love in other ways. When the family had financial problems, Bronislawa took it upon herself to make shoes by hand to save money. She taught Manya that there is no shame in hard manual labor. Years later, Manya would not think twice about undertaking backbreaking work in order to complete scientific experiments.

When Manya was a small child, Bronislawa suddenly refused to kiss or hug her children. The little girl didn't understand why her mother was no longer affectionate with her. The children didn't know it, but Bronislawa had contracted tuberculosis, a highly contagious disease. Although no one knew how tuberculosis was spread, Bronislawa would not take any chances of passing it to her children. So she stopped touching them altogether.

From that time on, Bronislawa searched for a cure. When Manya was five years old, Bronislawa and Manya's oldest sister, Zofia, left home to take a rest cure in the country. For the next few years the two traveled to different areas where it was thought that the clean air would cure Bronislawa's disease. Eventually they would return home, only to set out once more when she became ill again.

It was during one of these visits home that another blow befell the family. In 1874 an epidemic of a disease called typhus spread through the city and Zofia died. The death rocked the family. Four years later, on May 9, 1878, Manya's mother died as well. Manya was devastated. She became depressed, and her schoolwork suffered. The whole family was despondent. Gradually, however, the family began to recover. Manya once again focused on her schoolwork. But she never forgot her beloved mother or the sister who never had a chance to grow up. For the rest of her life she remembered the sorrow of their deaths.

MANYA EXCELS AT SCHOOL

Home and school were always intertwined in Manya's life. Lessons and playtime were one and the same. By the time Manya began formal school, she had already been exposed to history, science, languages, poetry, and geography at home.

Manya could be very serious about her work, but she was also kind and friendly. Although she was the youngest in the class, the other students regularly asked Manya to help them with mathematics and other difficult subjects.

School in Poland under Russian control was, at times, confusing. In many schools the staff taught subjects, such as Polish history and language, which were forbidden by the Russian government. Manya's school was no different. To hide this forbidden curriculum, the teachers drew up false class descriptions and schedules that made it appear that they were teaching the government-required Russian classes. They gave these false schedules to the Russian officials.

Sometimes, however, the Russians would make a surprise visit to the school. When that happened, the teachers and students had to hide all of their Polish materials and speak Russian instead. If anyone made a mistake, everyone in the school could be arrested. Manya and her classmates felt the strain of this double life.

Manya's teachers quickly realized how smart Manya was and how well she spoke Russian, so it was little Manya who usually recited the lessons when the dreaded Russian inspectors came to class. Manya never forgot how deeply she hated these displays. She was very shy, and the pressure of performing for the Russian officials always angered her. For the rest of her life, Manya never got over her distaste of speaking in public.

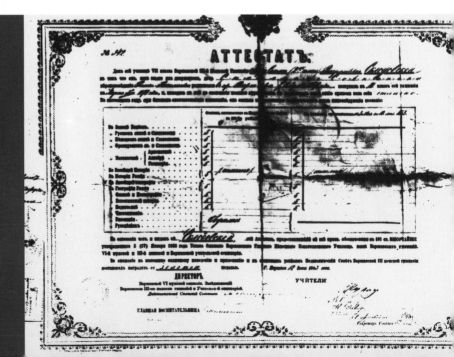

Manya was an exceptional student. Her favorite subjects included mathematics and the sciences, which her father also loved. She received this diploma when she graduated first in her class in 1883.

When Manya was eleven she enrolled in a gymnasium similar to the one where her father had once taught. She wrote, "In spite of everything, I like school. Perhaps you will make fun of me, but nevertheless I must tell you that I like it, and even that I love it." She remained at the gymnasium for five years and graduated on June 12, 1883. She was the first in her class, receiving the prized gold medal. She won awards in mathematics, history, literature, German, English, and French, as well as the heavy gold medal. Finally, when the ceremony was over, Manya happily left the gymnasium for good. She was just fifteen years old.

Amid her family's joy at her graduation, Manya felt confused. School was over forever, and she wasn't sure what was next. It was time to decide what she would do for the rest of her life.

Launching a Dream

As a girl, Manya's options for future education were limited. She could choose to become a teacher in private schools, or she could leave her beloved Poland to study abroad in Paris, France, or St. Petersburg, Russia.

There were more troubling issues in Manya's life, however. She was worn out and ill. No one knew for sure what was wrong. For her entire life Manya would feel ill, and sometimes collapse, during times of extreme stress. Vladyslaw saw how ill his youngest daughter had become, so he made a decision: Manya would live with relatives in the country for a year. She was ecstatic. For the young girl who had worked so hard, a year in the country seemed like heaven.

THE VACATION OF A LIFETIME

Soon after graduation, Manya boarded a train for the country manor houses of her uncles Henryk and Wladyskaw Boguski in southern Poland. Her uncles filled their homes with books, music, art, and conversation, and Manya blossomed. In a letter to a friend Manya described the fun she was having on her vacation. Apart from an hour's French lesson with a local student, she had all of her time for herself. She read novels instead of academic works, took long walks in the woods with friends and relatives, played on swings, swam as much as she liked, and went fishing.

In the fall, Manya traveled to the boisterous household of her uncle Zdzislaw and aunt Maria. They welcomed their niece warmly into the family. Evening parties filled the house with laughter and excitement. Manya had never enjoyed herself so much in her life.

PARTIES AND FUN

By far the most exciting parties were the kuligs. A kulig was a traditional Polish party. At night, large groups of people loaded onto horse-drawn sleighs and drove to a neighbor's house. The owner of the house pretended to be surprised as dozens of people tumbled inside, laughing and talking. Soon musicians were playing lively tunes and mounds of food were brought out. After a time, the guests climbed back into their sleighs and moved to the next house, then the next. Polish kuligs could last for days.

Manya wrote exuberant letters to friends and family describing the excitement of the kuligs she attended. Everyone wore beautiful clothes, including herself, she said. She talked about dancing the night away with a succession of handsome boys. Some nights they danced until morning.

Eventually the kuligs ended, and the winter turned to spring. Manya left her relatives and went to visit Madame de Fleury, a former student of Manya's mother. She and her husband owned a luxurious country estate, known as Kepa. Manya's sister Helena was also invited. Years later, Helena would write that that summer was the best time of her entire life. Manya felt the same way. The two sisters had the freedom to do whatever they liked.

Manya was depressed and exhausted when she left school. Her year in the country revived her spirits and was the only carefree year of her life. Here, she poses with the de Fleury family and friends at the family estate in 1884.

Sometimes they slept during the day if the mood took them. They danced, ran, and came up with wild schemes that kept the entire household on their toes. The girls delighted in playing practical jokes on everyone in the house. No one was safe.

Finally Manya's yearlong vacation came to an end. Both Manya and Helena cherished the memory of that summer. Helena wrote that the summer passed quickly, but the memory of it would last forever. When they grew old, Helena and Manya would fondly recall their time at Kepa and the crazy summer they had there.

SECRET STUDIES AT THE FLYING UNIVERSITY

Manya returned home to Warsaw to face even more troubles than when she had left. Her father's health had worsened. Financial problems plagued the family. Much of the family's money went to Jozef, who was a medical student at the University of Warsaw. Bronya ran the household, but she dreamed of becoming a doctor.

To make money, Manya began tutoring students. In her spare time she studied as much as she could and wrote in her journal. She longed for new ideas and intellectual stimulation that dry books alone could not give her.

She found it in a secret school. It was known as the Flying University because the classes moved from place to place. At the time, Polish universities would not admit women, so girls had little opportunity for advanced study. The university was held in private homes all around the city. It offered classes in such courses as anatomy, natural history, and sociology. By the time Manya entered the Flying University, more than a thousand women were enrolled.

Studying among dozens of other intelligent, ambitious women, Manya was exposed to new ideas. However, even the Flying University couldn't quench Manya's thirst for knowledge. She wanted to go to a real university, but how?

MANYA AND BRONYA HATCH A PLAN

One day Manya approached Bronya with a bold idea. Bronya would enroll in university in Paris, using the money she'd saved to survive the first year. Manya would find a job as a governess. Manya would send Bronya money every month. When Bronya became a doctor, it would be Manya's turn to go. Bronya agreed to the plan. That October, the whole family went to the train station to see Bronya off to Paris. Manya had found a job as a governess, so soon after Bronya's departure Manya left to start her part of the bargain.

Manya's first job was a disaster. She strongly disliked the family who

Both Manya (left) and Bronya were determined to continue their educations. This photo was taken in 1886, when Manya was nineteen. At the time she had been working as a governess to finance Bronya's medical school education.

had hired her and disapproved of their lifestyle. She wrote that the family lived as though they were rich, but they really didn't pay their bills for months. Instead, they spent their money on frivilous pleasures while at the same time skimping on necessities. She left after only a few weeks.

Soon she found a better job. It was a three-year contract that paid 500 rubles a year—a nice amount for a young governess. But it was far away, in the small country village of Szczuki. As much as Manya wanted to be near her family, she decided to accept the job. The day she left on her journey remained one of the clearest, and saddest, memories of Manya's life. Her heart felt heavy as she boarded the train. She knew she would be traveling hundreds of miles away from everyone she loved most in the world. Manya was full of apprehension, fearful that this new family would be as bad as the

Life as a Governess

Governesses were usually hired by well-to-do families to teach their girls at home, since most girls were not allowed to attend school. Like Manya, most governesses were well-educated themselves, and they taught subjects such as reading, writing, mathematics, languages, geography, and history.

Life as a governess was sometimes difficult. Many young women left their own families for the first time to live with their employers, just as Manya did. A governess was expected to have the education and manners of a "lady," but was usually treated like a servant. The life of a governess was often isolated and lonely. Most governesses, however, endured their jobs, because there were no other jobs for middle-class, educated women.

one before. But this time she could not leave so easily. What was in store for her? she wondered.

Fortunately, Manya's new employers, the Zorawskis, were much better than the first ones. Manya felt welcome in their home, and the family treated her with kindness and respect. She made friends with the eldest daughter, Bronka, and this friendship made it easier for Manya to settle into her new life. Manya's pupil, Andzia, was a sweet child but also very spoiled. Manya was determined to teach Andzia her subjects and to instill some manners in the wild, unruly girl.

Being a good employee was not Manya's only goal. She insisted on keeping up with her own studies. When her duties as governess were over for the day, Manya studied physics, sociology, and anatomy, wrote letters, and worked complicated math problems for pleasure. She did not want to be too far behind when she finally went back to school—if she ever did.

BITTER ENDINGS AND NEW BEGINNINGS

Sometime during the first part of her three-year stay with the Zorawski family, Manya met the Zorawskis' eldest son, Kazimierz. He was a year older than Manya, studying mathematics at the University of Warsaw. He was an intelligent, handsome young man. Kazimierz saw in Manya a young, attractive woman who could dance, who loved boating and skating, who had a wicked sense of humor, and who was opinionated and intelligent. Eventually Manya and Kazimierz fell in love and decided to marry.

The young couple assumed that their plans would be welcomed by both families, but when Kazimierz's parents found out, they were furious. As much as they liked Manya, she was still a penniless governess in their eyes. They refused to agree to the marriage. Manya was heartbroken, especially when Kazimierz went along with his parents' wishes to end the relationship. Manya was soured on romance. Never again, she promised herself.

Worse, she could not leave because she was still supporting Bronya in school, so she remained as governess with the family. Life returned to normal, but Manya had changed as a result of her bitter experience. She continued to treat the family as she always had, but her affection for them had disappeared. Manya became lonely and depressed. Living in isolation with the family who had rejected her and being far from her own family and friends took a heavy toll on Manya, who once had such romantic dreams of her future. Her letters to her brother, Jozef, were filled with despair. She had lost hope in ever leaving the profession and making something of herself, she said. All of her ambitions were for her brother and sisters, she wrote, and she was filled with regret for her decisions. But there was nothing to do about them now.

Manya endured the rest of her time with the Zorawskis as best she could. Finally, in the spring of 1889, Manya left the tiny village of Szczuki for good. She had found a new job with another family on the Baltic coast. By now Manya was twenty-two and had

Manya fell deeply in love with the Zorawski's dashing, intelligent son Kazimierz. Although he broke their engagement at his family's request, the couple may have continued the romance in secret until Manya left for Paris.

resigned herself to a life as a governess. Her youthful dreams of study were all but forgotten beneath the weight of responsibility.

THE DREAM BEGINS

In March of 1890, Manya received an unexpected letter from Bronya. "And now you, my little Manya," Bronya wrote, "If you can get together a few hundred rubles this year you can come to Paris next year and live with us. . . . It is absolutely necessary to have a few hundred rubles for your fee at the Sorbonne [a Paris university]. . . . You must take this decision, you have been waiting too long. I guarantee that in two years you will have your master's degree."

It was the invitation Manya had once longed for, but by now she had lost all hope of getting an education. Now that her dream had been handed back to her, she didn't know what to do. The two sisters argued through letters for months. Then at the end of the summer in 1891, Bronya got the letter she had been waiting for. "Decide if you can really take me in your house, for I can come now," Manya wrote. "I have enough to pay all my expenses. If, therefore, without depriving yourself of a great deal, you could give me my food, write to me and say so. It would be a great happiness."

Bronya immediately wrote back and told her to come. At the end of September 1891, Manya boarded a train for Paris and a new life.

Marie's Paris was a vibrant city. Painters such as Camille Pissaro captured the excitement in works such as *The Boulevard Montmartre, Paris.*

THREE

A Student in Paris

Paris was everything Manya had dreamed of. Paris at the end of the 1800s was a bright, exciting city. The streets teemed with fashionable ladies and gentlemen, all hurrying to and fro along the cobbled streets. Delicious smells wafted from every sidewalk café Manya passed by. The twin towers of the great Notre Dame cathedral rose over the Seine River, casting their shadow on the famous waterway that wound through the heart of Paris. The din of horses, carriages, and people filled the air from morning until night. It was all sometimes overwhelming, but Manya took it in like a prisoner who had been unexpectedly set free. She could browse the sidewalk book vendors or buy a loaf of crusty, warm bread and wander wherever she liked. Manya was just one small foreign girl in the huge city, but for the first time in a long time she felt young, powerful, and in control of her life.

While in Paris, Bronya had met and married a Polish man named Kazimierz Dluski. He was a tall, handsome man that Manya would come to call "my little brother-in-law." He met her at the station and took her to their small second-floor apartment in a working-class area of Paris.

Marie often walked past the famous Notre Dame cathedral as she explored Paris. Today the cathedral still towers over the Seine River in Paris, just as it did when Marie first came to the city.

The apartment was small but warm and comfortable. The newlyweds had furnished it with second-hand furniture purchased at auctions. The bookshelves were filled with Polish volumes, Polish pictures hung on the walls, and only Polish was spoken in the house. Manya could feel at home while adjusting to life in Paris.

She had arrived early, so she could enjoy the city and get her bearings before classes started in November. Manya strolled through the Paris avenues, marveling at everything she saw. In the early morning the streets were full of people: women carrying every kind of food imaginable to market; merchants surrounded by baskets of flowers and other goods, butchers groaning under the weight of huge slabs of meat they carried. It was all strange, new, and wonderful.

Manya was filled with the heady taste of intellectual and political freedom for the first time in her life. In Poland there were books she could

Paris in the 1890s

In the 1890s Manya's Paris was one of the most exciting, progressive cities in the world. Only two years before she arrived, the grand Eiffel Tower had been opened for the International Exposition of 1889. Its revolutionary new look had never before been seen anywhere. Radical Impressionist artists such as Claude Monet and Mary Cassatt broke from traditional art styles and created entirely new kinds of paintings. Another artist, Henri de Toulouse-Lautrec, spent his nights at the Moulin Rouge Cabaret and created astonishingly fresh art that made the Moulin Rouge can-can dancers famous. The Lumière brothers were showing their new invention, moving pictures, to sold-out audiences. The thrill of the new and exciting was everywhere, and Manya was a part of it.

not read, things she could not say, even thoughts she felt she was not allowed to think. In Paris she was free to speak, think, and read anything she wanted. This freedom gave Manya a new strength and determination to succeed. She was in Paris, she was young, and she was free!

GOING TO UNIVERSITY

On the first day of class, Manya set out for the Sorbonne, the university that she would be attending. The Sorbonne was one of the most progressive schools in Europe. It admitted female students, which was rare for any European university. Students could choose which classes to attend, how often to go to class, and when they took the exams to graduate.

Manya registered for classes, choosing courses in physics and calculus in the Faculty of Science department. When she signed her name in the

By the time Marie enrolled in school, the Sorbonne was one of the most respected universities in Europe. Today the Sorbonne continues to attract students from around the world.

registry, she took the French style of her name, "Marie Sklodowski." From that time on, she was known as Marie.

When classes began, Manya, now Marie, was alarmed to discover that she was much less prepared than she thought. Although she had done her best to keep up with her studies, she realized that she did not have the mathematical skills to understand university-level science classes. As a result, Marie found it very hard to keep up with the other students. Marie also quickly realized that her French was not at all as good as she expected. During class, if a professor got excited and spoke too quickly, Marie lost entire sentences. Marie got into the habit of arriving at class early so that she could get a good seat up front, where she could see the chalkboard and hear the lecture more clearly.

The first few weeks flew by. She spent as much time as she could at school, then used her evenings for study. Slowly she began to grasp the complex mathematics

The Sorbonne

Marie's school, the Sorbonne, had a long history. In 1257 Robert de Sorbon began a college for students who had no money to pay for their education. Students at the time were expected to follow a tough course of classes, including theology, astronomy, grammar, and mathematics. Later the school became the foundation for the University of Paris. Eventually the university grew to include more than forty different colleges, but the Sorbonne remained the most famous and respected. Today the name "Sorbonne" is sometimes used to refer to the entire University of Paris system.

needed for her classes, and her French improved. She loved going to class every day, hearing the science lectures, and then becoming lost in her schoolbooks far into the night.

MARIE STRIKES OUT ON HER OWN

After a few months living with Bronya and Kazimierz, Marie realized that she needed a place of her own. The long commute was taking a toll on her finances and her study time. Also, Bronya and Kazimierz's life was full of distractions for the young student. Visitors rang the apartment bell at all hours of the evening, patients came in and out, and there was little peace. Kazimierz might suddenly acquire theater tickets and insist that Marie go along. All Marie wanted to do was study.

Marie decided to find her own lodging closer to the Sorbonne. She searched among the tiny rooms in the area usually rented to students and found one to her liking. It was small, cheap, and near the school. It was everything Marie needed.

Even though Marie moved frequently during her student years, all of the rooms

Marie posed for this sketch in 1892 while she was a student in Paris. A fellow student captured her simple clothing and her intense gaze. These characteristics would define Marie for the rest of her life.

The Light She Longs to Find

Although student life was difficult, Marie always looked back on her student days as some of the best years of her life. She wrote a poem about how she felt, capturing both the loneliness and the joy of being on her own. The last stanza reads:

> *It is the light she longs to find,*
> *When she delights in learning more,*
> *Her world is learning; it defines*
> *The destiny she's reaching for.*

she lived in looked the same. They were almost always on the top floor of an older building, because the attic rooms were usually the cheapest. These rooms were under the eaves, which meant Marie would sweat through high temperatures in summer and would freeze during the winter. The room usually had only one window or skylight. Marie owned a few pieces of scuffed furniture, including a table, a chair, a trunk for her clothes, a washbasin and a pitcher for water, a coal scuttle, an oil lamp, an iron folding bed, a mattress, and bedding. It was not much, but it was hers.

MARIE'S LIFE AS A STUDENT

The Sorbonne was the perfect place to be a science student in the late 1800s, and Marie was able to take advantage of it. The curriculum was structured with a new emphasis on science and technology instruction.

Marie spent all day listening to lectures or working in the school's laboratory. In the evenings she trudged home and up the steep flights of stairs to her sparsely furnished room. She ate a modest meal and studied far into the night by the light of a single oil lamp. If it was cold, she put on every piece of clothing she owned. It was a solitary life, but Marie loved it.

In 1893, two years after Marie first set out for Paris, she was ready to take her exams. For all of the preparation Marie had done, all the study, the endless lonely nights, she was still very nervous at the thought of the exams. After the exams, she waited for days until the results were announced. Then she got astounding news. Marie had not only passed her exams, but she placed first in her class. More important, Marie Sklodowski had become the first woman to receive a physics degree at the Sorbonne.

UNEXPECTED MONEY AND A NEW GOAL

Elated, Marie traveled home to Warsaw to visit her father and to relax from the last two years of hard work and study. While she was there, she received news that she had been awarded a 600 ruble scholarship, which would be worth about $5,000 today. That much money would support Marie in Paris for months. She decided to return to the Sorbonne to persue a second degree, this time in mathematics. So at the end of the summer of 1893, Marie returned to Paris a few weeks early to prepare for a new round of classes at the Sorbonne. As much as she had enjoyed the time she spent with her family, she was delighted to be back in Paris. Ever the student, Marie spent the few weeks before classes began studying mathematics so that she wouldn't be behind. She realized what a precious gift this year of study was, and she had no intention of wasting it.

It did not take Marie long to achieve this next goal. In the summer of 1894, she passed her exams for the *licence es mathématiques* and ranked second in her class. She was now twenty-six years old, and her credentials ensured that she could easily find a position as a respected teacher in Warsaw, which she intended to do. The future she had dreamed of so long ago with Bronya had finally come true.

By the time Marie graduated from the Sorbonne, she was determined to return to Poland and become a teacher. Instead, she remained in Paris and began her career as a scientist. This photo was taken in 1903, the year she won her first Nobel prize.

FOUR

A New Life

In 1894, while Marie was still a student, she had been hired by the Society for the Encouragement of National Industry to conduct a scientific study of the magnetic properties of different steels. It was a paying job, and Marie jumped at the chance to do her own scientific study. She began the project in the laboratory of one of her professors, but she soon realized that she would need a larger space.

A possible solution to the dilemma came from an unlikely place. She mentioned her problem to some of her friends. They had an idea. A scientist and teacher they knew might have a free workroom at the School of Physics and Chemistry in Paris. Marie agreed to meet the scientist to discuss the possibility. The scientist's name was Pierre Curie.

A GREAT SCIENTIST'S EARLY LIFE

Pierre Curie was born in Paris in May 1859. Like Marie's parents, the Curies had progressive ideas about education. They thought that children should be taught according to their individual strengths and desires. The Curies realized that their young son would not be happy in a formal school setting, so they decided to teach Pierre and his younger brother, Jacques, at home.

It was in this unheated, tumbledown storage room where Marie and Pierre conducted their ground-breaking experiments with radioactivity. This building is known as the "Shed of Discovery."

Pierre Curie was a respected scientist and professor when Marie met him in Paris. Although Pierre was much older than Marie, they shared a love for scientific exploration and experimentation.

Pierre's father, Eugène, let Pierre learn at his own pace. He took the boys on long vacations in the country, sharing his love of nature and his ideas about science as they tramped through the woods or lingered by a pond. Pierre grew up in awe of science and nature. He developed an unquenchable thirst to learn more and to understand how science worked.

Pierre's parents understood that their dreamy son needed a different style of education from most students. They didn't force him to study from books, but instead to learn from nature and the natural world. Years later a fellow scientist and friend, Paul Langevin, described Pierre's early education as "quite irregular." But it gave the young Pierre plenty of time to look closely at everything around him with his own eyes. Pierre formed a bond with nature that lasted throughout his lifetime. He learned to respect nature and the lessons it could teach, such as patience. Pierre's education, as Paul said, "rendered him incapable of this hasty, superficial, and insipid understanding one acquires from books."

Even though he did not have a formal education, Pierre easily passed all the exams he needed for entry into the Sorbonne. He completed his *licence es science* and began working as a scientific assistant at the University of Paris. Through the years he rose in the ranks, eventually becoming a professor in his own right. All the time he continued to study, to experiment, and to publish scientific papers.

When Marie met Pierre, he was already internationally known for his work with crystals, electricity, and magnetism. He had also invented a number of finely tuned scientific instruments that he used in his work. His published papers had earned him the respect of his fellow scientists and had paved the way for some important discoveries in magnetism.

Pierre, however, was an outsider in the French scientific community. When he graduated, he chose to take an assistant's position rather than to continue his studies. He had never received a Ph.D. in science, which was the highest achievement at the time. The school where he taught was not the most prestigious in the university. Although he was an accomplished scientist, Pierre refused to accept any awards and honors, consistently declining any opportunities that would make him more visible or better known in the scientific community. Money was not important to him, except for what he needed to continue his research. Because of that, he did not seek better paying jobs or positions with more respect or prestige. These things gave him a reputation of being eccentric and somewhat difficult.

Pierre, at thirty-five, had also sworn off love. He did not have a very high opinion of women when he wrote in his diary, "Women of genius are rare. . . . Thus, when we . . . give all our thoughts to some work which

Science in the 1800s

Marie and Pierre lived at a time when it was exciting to be a scientist. In 1868 Louis Pasteur discovered that bacteria causes disease, which eventually led to a revolution in medicine. Joseph Lister developed his ideas of clean surgery and antiseptics in the mid-1800s, which resulted in a dramatic drop in deaths from infection and unclean hospital conditions. In 1871 Charles Darwin published *Descent of Man*, changing the way humans understood their own distant past. In the late 1870s, Thomas Edison came up with his electric lightbulb. All of these scientific advances would eventually change the world.

estranges us from the humanity nearest us, we have to struggle against women."

This, of course, was before he met Marie.

A LIFELONG COLLABORATION BEGINS

On the day Marie entered the room at the boardinghouse where her friends were meeting for tea, she was immediately drawn to the quiet, brilliant older man. Marie described what she thought the moment she saw him, "I was struck by the expression of his clear gaze and by a slight appearance of carelessness in his lofty stature. His rather slow, reflective words, his simplicity, and his smile, at once grave and young, inspired confidence."

They both soon realized that the other was unlike anyone they had ever met. Marie was impressed by Pierre's brilliance and his kindness. Pierre was astonished, and pleased, to find a woman he could talk to about complex scientific issues. They also

Marie and Pierre posed for this photograph soon after their marriage in 1895. Pierre had decided that he would never marry, thinking that a wife would distract him from his scientific work. Marie changed his mind.

discovered that they shared similar opinions on politics, religion, and social issues.

Soon Pierre and Marie began spending a great deal of time with one another. They talked endlessly about science, government, politics, and their families. In the spring they took long walks together in the countryside. It was during those outings that Pierre introduced Marie to his love of nature. They both delighted in the beauty of the natural world. They were falling in love.

DIFFICULT CHOICES FOR MARIE

During this time Marie was working to complete her degree in mathematics. Her goals were clear: to complete her degree and to return to her family in Poland. She had not considered that a tall, quiet scientist would enter her world, but she was determined not to let love interfere with her life. When she graduated with her degree in mathematics in June 1894, she set out for a summer with her family in Switzerland and Poland, leaving Pierre behind in Paris.

Sometime before she left, Pierre had proposed marriage. As much as she loved Pierre, the idea of abandoning her beloved Poland to marry a Frenchman horrified her. To Marie it would be the same as renouncing her allegiance to Poland, and to do that would be, for her, a betrayal of her beloved country and her family.

Throughout that summer, wherever Marie went, letters from Pierre followed. He knew that her love of her family and of Poland was strong and that it would take his best efforts to woo her back to Paris. He constantly wrote of his affection for her, and he did not hesitate to tell her how delighted he was whenever he got a letter from her. He reminded her that they shared so much, writing, "It would be a fine thing . . . to pass our lives near each other, hypnotized by our dreams; your patriotic dream, our humanitarian dream and our scientific dream."

None of Marie's correspondence to Pierre during this time survives, so there is no way to know what she said to him throughout that long summer of letters. Something must have convinced Marie, for she finally agreed to return to Paris in the fall. Pierre could hardly contain his joy.

Ten more months passed before Marie made the difficult choice to marry Pierre and remain in Paris. It was not easy for her to come to this decision. Her brother Jozef reassured her. He told her that he thought she was right to follow her heart. If she did, he said, no one could complain. Although she was marrying a Frenchman, Jozef assured her that she would remain Polish, no matter what.

Pierre wrote many letters like this one to Marie while she was in Poland in the summer of 1894. Although Marie desperately wanted to live in Poland with her family, she finally chose a life with Pierre instead.

Marie and Pierre loved the freedom of traveling by bicycle. Here, they pose for the camera with the new bicycles they purchased for their honeymoon. For the rest of their lives they spent summers in the country, riding bikes and exploring the countryside.

FIRST DAYS OF A NEW LIFE

On July 26, 1895, Marie and Pierre were married quietly in the town hall of the small French town of Sceaux. Afterward there was a reception in the Curie family garden a short distance away. The two families ate, played games, and congratulated the new couple. Then Marie and Pierre set off on an unusual honeymoon, a bicycling trip. They had purchased brand-new bicycles and were anxious to explore the countryside.

Marie fondly recalled the honeymoon trip for the rest of her life. These quiet, happy days were filled with nothing but one another. They formed a strong bond that went beyond husband and wife, beyond scientific equals. They became partners in every sense of the word. They inspired one another, and they both looked to their future life together with joy and excitement.

IDEAS AND DISCOVERIES

Once the idyllic honeymoon was over, Marie and Pierre returned to Paris. They found a small apartment in the city and furnished it sparsely. Neither of them had time for housework. Pierre was still employed at the university, and Marie was continuing her paid research on magnetism and steel. She also returned to studying because she had decided to take the exams that were required to become a teacher.

Soon Marie and Pierre were expecting their first child. Irène Curie was born on September 12, 1897. Now Marie had to juggle home life with her scientific career. By this time, she had completed her study on magnetism and steel and was preparing to publish her results. She had also taken her exams to become a teacher. Motherhood did not deter Marie from her ambitions. She and Pierre decided that Marie should reach even higher—she should begin work on her Ph.D., the most prestigious degree one could receive in France.

Bicycles:

THE NEW CRAZE

When Marie and Pierre got married, France and the rest of the world were swept up in a craze for bicycles. Bicycles revolutionized transportation. At first they were faddish toys for the rich, but ordinary people soon realized that bicycles gave them newfound freedom. People organized bicycle travel clubs. Young people could escape the prying eyes of adults. Bicycles gave women the freedom to go where they pleased, and young couples like Pierre and Marie could travel through the country on romantic bicycle vacations.

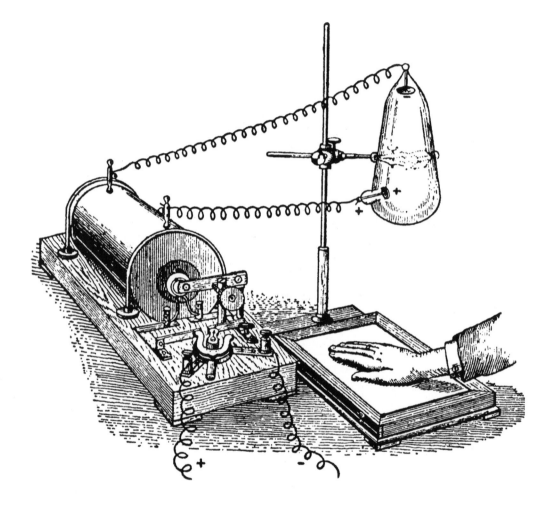

This sketch illustrates one of the first X ray machines. When Marie and Pierre began their scientific experiments, X rays were a new and exciting discovery.

FIVE

The Great Discovery

Once Curie decided to pursue a Ph.D., she tackled it with the same dogged resolve she had shown as a student at the Sorbonne. One of the requirements was to conduct original research in a specific scientific field. She wanted to choose a topic that interested her, and she was determined to pick a subject that no one else had researched. Marie spent many hours poring through scientific journals and discussing different ideas with Pierre. Finally she settled on a study of a little-understood phenomenon: compounds that contained the element uranium gave off strange rays, similar to X rays. It would lead to the discovery of a lifetime.

STRANGE RAYS AND URANIUM

The series of scientific events that led Curie to her life's work began in 1895. In November of that year, a German scientist named Wilhelm Roentgen was experimenting with vacuum tubes and electricity. When he covered the tube with cardboard, then charged it with electricity, he produced rays that made a special screen across the room glow. He called his new discovery "X rays."

Roentgen and his X rays became instantly famous all over the world. A French scientist, Antoine Henri Becquerel, was especially interested in the fact that these rays caused objects to phosphoresce, or glow. He began experimenting on his own to discover more about the strange glowing effect.

During his experiments he stumbled on something even more odd. In one experiment he put uranium salts on a photographic plate wrapped in black paper, then exposed it to the sun. An image of the salt

A Famous First X Ray

On December 22, 1895, Wilhelm Roentgen was experimenting in his laboratory. The new, strange "X" rays that he had just discovered had seized his imagination. He tried to x-ray anything he could find. Roentgen made an X-ray photograph of his wife's right hand, along with a ring she wore on her finger. Although this X ray was not the only one he made during this time, it is now traditionally known as the world's first X-ray picture.

crystals appeared on the photographic plate. He believed that it was the sun that had caused the image to appear on the photographic plate through the paper.

He wanted to try the experiment again. He put a copper cross between the paper and the uranium salts, but by the time he was ready, it had become cloudy outside. Becquerel put the paper-wrapped photographic plate in a dark cabinet. A few days later, Becquerel decided to develop the photographic plate anyway. To his astonishment, there was a clear image of the copper cross on the negative! The uranium salts didn't need the sunlight to create an image on the plate. Becquerel realized that the uranium salts were producing some kind of new rays that penetrated the paper, even in complete darkness.

Becquerel's rays did not capture the imagination of the world as X rays had done. Only one other scientist, William Thomson, also known as Lord Kelvin, was interested in the subject. He conducted some experiments and achieved similar results. He believed that X rays and uranium rays somehow "electrified" the air, causing the glow, but the door was still open to further study.

THE DISCOVERY

Curie needed somewhere to do her research. The School of Physics and Chemistry, where Pierre taught, eventually agreed to give Marie a small, glassed-in room in which to work. The space was little more than a storage room and machine shop, with no heat and only a few rickety tables. It was damp, badly lit, and the roof sometimes leaked, but Curie gladly accepted the offer. It wasn't much, but it was hers.

Curie's first step was to answer some intriguing questions: What was the energy in uranium? Where did it come from? Did any other substance "electrify the air" as uranium did? She began by testing as many samples of different metals and minerals as she could find. For weeks, Marie methodically tested dozens of compounds and minerals.

On February 17, 1898, she tested a sample of a compound called pitchblende. Pitchblende was a source of uranium, but it was considered to be worthless after the uranium was extracted. Much to Curie's amazement, the pitchblende caused a much stronger current than uranium alone had done. At first Curie thought her equipment was faulty. After days of testing her instruments, she realized they were all working fine. Then she tested the pitchblende again and got the same astounding results. The next few days were spent testing other materials against the pitchblende, and Curie got another surprise. She found that the mineral eschynite also gave off stronger rays than uranium.

Curie realized that these rays weren't caused by some outside energy force or the sun or even the compounds themselves. She deduced that they must be coming from some other source deep inside the compounds. She had already tested all known chemical elements.

Pitchblende, shown here, is a brownish-black rock that is made primarily of uranium. During Marie's time, pitchblende was considered to be a worthless byproduct of uranium mining.

Radiation and Radioactivity

Marie had discovered a new kind of "ray," which she would eventually call "radioactivity." Radioactivity is the spontaneous disintegration of the nucleus of an atom, which releases energy, much of it as radiation, which are the strange "rays" that Marie first recorded. Today, scientists classify radiation into three categories, which are alpha particles, beta particles, and gamma rays.

The only explanation must be that some new element, something that no one had discovered, was causing the rays.

Curie was excited and shocked, but also sensible. Now she must prove conclusively that what she had stumbled on was indeed a new element. Pierre was also intrigued by Marie's findings. He decided to set aside his own research and help his wife with her experiments.

As a team they set to work with renewed effort. Slowly they separated the active parts of the compounds, creating a compound that was hundreds of time stronger than uranium. By July 1898—only five months after Marie's accidental discovery of the rays in pitchblende—the Curies concluded that the only explanation was that they had indeed discovered a new element.

That month they wrote a paper titled "On a New Radioactive Substance Contained in Pitchblende." It was the first time anyone had used the word radioactive. It was also the moment when they named their new element "polonium." The Curies wrote, "We have obtained a substance which

Marie and Pierre spent almost all of their time in their "lab," the storage room at the School of Physics and Chemistry. Soon after Marie accidentally discovered radiation, Pierre decided to abandon his own work to help Marie.

is 400 times as active as uranium. . . . We thus believe that this substance we have extracted from pitchblende contains a metal not yet reported. . . . If the existence of this metal is confirmed, we propose to call it polonium after the name of the country of origin of one of us."

A BIGGER SURPRISE

There was something else in the pitchblende besides polonium. During their experimentation Marie and Pierre became convinced that there was not one, but two new elements that gave off the strong rays. After more experimentation they thought they had found it. By December they had prepared a second paper announcing their findings. On December 26, 1898, it was presented to the French Academy of Sciences, the most respected scientific organization in France at the time.

Part of the paper, called "On a New, Strongly Radioactive Substance, Contained in Pitchblende" read, "The various reasons we have just enumerated lead us to believe that the new radioactive substance contains a new element to which we propose to give the name of RADIUM. The new radioactive substance certainly contains a very strong proportion of barium; in spite of that, its radioactivity is considerable. The radioactivity of radium ought therefore to be enormous."

MARIE PROVES HER DISCOVERY

Announcing the discovery of what they believed to be a new element was one thing. Proving it existed was something else entirely. Both Marie and Pierre were already convinced that radium and polonium existed. Now they had to convince the rest of the scientific community that they had discovered not one, but two new elements. The only way to do that, Curie realized, was to isolate them.

She knew it would be a huge undertaking, especially with the substandard conditions of the storage room/lab she and Pierre were still laboring in. But the thought of the hard work didn't scare her. Years before, her parents, especially her mother, had taught Marie the value of hard work. She knew she would have to do it alone, because she and Pierre had no staff, no money, and a work space that was substandard at best. But Curie didn't hesitate. She had no fear of throwing herself into the work in order to isolate the new elements.

They quickly realized that they needed hundreds of pounds of pitchblende to extract even the tiniest amounts of radium. Through their contacts at the university they discovered that a uranium mine in Austria had tons of pitchblende waste. The Austrian government agreed to sell it to the Curies. Once it was delivered, the real work began.

Marie wasn't afraid of hard, tedious work. She knew it would take months to isolate the new element she had discovered. Although the conditions in their storage-room lab were terrible, Marie was convinced she could do it.

For the next four years Curie painstakingly worked to isolate the radium from the pitchblende. It was backbreaking labor. She boiled, stirred, and mixed a variety of chemicals with the pitchblende, spending hours in the poorly ventilated, dimly lit lab. Curie would sometimes spend an entire day stirring thick, boiling mixtures with a huge iron rod almost as big as she was. By nighttime, she collapsed into bed from exhaustion.

Some days the entire batch became contaminated with dirt or dust, and she would have to throw it all away and begin again. Other days it was too cold, or too hot, in the lab to work properly. Instruments broke down and had to be replaced or repaired. Noxious fumes from the chemicals made it difficult to breathe. When it rained, Curie had to move her equipment so that the leaky roof would not damage or contaminate anything.

Slowly, however, the new element emerged from Curie's tedious work.

After thousands of hours of work and several tons of pitchblende, Curie finally isolated one decigram—one-tenth of gram, which is 0.035 ounce—of almost pure radium chloride.

During her long days working in the lab, as she created more pure concentrations of radium, she was delighted to discover that radium glowed with a strange luminescence. She wrote that they "had an especial joy in observing that our products containing concentrated radium were all spontaneously luminous. My husband . . . had to agree that this other unhoped-for characteristic gave him even greater satisfaction."

Sometimes, in the evening after the day's work was done, Marie and Pierre would steal back into the quiet, dark storeroom laboratory. They placed chairs facing the tables. Then they would sit, transfixed, watching the soft glow of the radium in the numerous tubes and bottles. "Our precious products," Marie wrote, "for which we had no shelter, were arranged on tables and boards; from all sides we could see their slightly luminous silhouettes, and these gleamings, which seemed suspended in the darkness, stirred us with ever new emotion and enchantment."

Although Marie and Pierre were virtually ignored by their French peers, the rest of the world began to take notice of them. They were regarded as two of the most remarkable scientists of their day.

The Nobel Prize, Fame, and Strange Ailments

Scientists around the world had already begun to take notice of the Curies's work in their ramshackle lab at the School of Physics and Chemistry. However, the French scientific community continued to snub the Curies, especially Pierre. In 1898 a position opened at the Sorbonne. Candidates had to be voted into the position, called a chair, in an election. Although Pierre did superior scientific work, many professors in the Sorbonne disliked him. Pierre lost the election.

This was a financial and professional blow to the Curies, for a chair at the Sorbonne meant not only more money, but better laboratory facilities. Marie had put aside her Ph.D. study to focus entirely on radium. Pierre still taught classes at the School of Physics and Chemistry, but the laboratory took up the rest of his time. They could manage on Pierre's small salary, but it would be difficult.

The word was spreading that something remarkable was happening in the drafty storeroom in Paris. A few organizations began to award them scientific prizes, which was a boost to their small income. Marie published more papers describing her ongoing work with radium, and she collaborated with Pierre on additional papers. The awards and scientific publications fueled interest in Marie's radium rays, which brought them more attention. Marie and Pierre were now regarded at the same level as other respected scientists around the world.

During this time a colleague, Henri Poincaré, managed to secure a teaching position for Pierre at the Sorbonne. Although it wasn't an official chair, it was a better-paying job than the one he had at the School of Physics and Chemistry. At the same time, Marie decided to accept a position on the faculty of the École Normale Supérieure at Sèvres, one of the best girls' schools in France. Marie was the first woman named to the faculty of the school, a great achievement at the time.

The new jobs eased their money troubles, but their additional responsibilities ate into their time in the lab. Marie continued her research whenever she could, between lectures, time with Irène, and the hundreds of small distractions of daily life. She resumed writing her dissertation for her Ph.D., which also required time and attention. Even with all of these new responsibilities, a great sense of happiness came to both Marie and Pierre. They were together, they were doing the work they loved, and they were making wonderful new discoveries about radium—their radium—in their lab.

DEFENDING HER WORK

In 1903 Curie finished writing her dissertation. The only step left was to present herself and her work before a panel of distinguished Sorbonne examiners. In June of 1903 she entered the students' hall of the Sorbonne to face the examiners. Pierre and his father, Eugène Curie, were there, as was her sister Bronya who had traveled from Poland, where she had moved, to support her "little Manya." Some of her students from Sèvres also attended to support their respected woman professor.

Curie calmly and purposefully defended her dissertation. She answered tough questions from the examiners and explained details of her research. At the end there was no question: Marie was awarded the title *docteur es sciences physiques* (doctor of physical sciences), with honors. Not only

Marie and Pierre welcomed their first child, daughter Irène, in 1897. Their experiments kept them busy, but they always found time for Irène. They took her on their country vacations, such as the one pictured here, in the summer of 1904.

Alfred Nobel and his Prizes

The idea of the Nobel Prizes came from Alfred Nobel, a successful businessman and engineer. Nobel invented dynamite in 1866. Later, he built companies and laboratories all over the world. He also invented more than three hundred different machines and devices. As a result, Nobel was among the richest men in the world.

Nobel soon realized the deadly potential of the dynamite he had invented. He created the Nobel Prizes as a way to promote peace and understanding among all people. The prizes are given every year to individuals who are considered to have made the greatest contributions benefiting all of humankind.

Marie and Pierre received this certificate for their Nobel prize for Physics in 1903. The certificate does not mention the Curies' discovery of polonium or radium, however. Instead, they were recognized, along with Henri Becquerel, for their work with radiation.

that, but the examiners stated that Curie's findings represented the greatest scientific contribution ever made in a doctoral thesis. It was a grand triumph for Curie and her work.

THE NOBEL PRIZE AND THE PRICE OF FAME

In August of 1903 the Nobel Prize committee at the Swedish Academy met to consider nominees for the prizes. These prizes, awarded to distinguished scientists, writers, and leaders throughout the world, represented the highest honor in each field. Over the past few months the committee had received letters recommending Marie and Pierre and their work on uranium.

By August the committee delivered its report to the physics section of the Swedish Academy. Part of the report said, "A completely new field of greatest importance and interest has opened up for physics research. . . . The credit for these discoveries belongs without a doubt in the first place to Henri Becquerel and to M. and Mme. Curie. . . . The discovery by Becquerel of the spontaneous radioactivity of uranium. . . . Inspired diligent research to find other elements with similar remarkable qualities. The most magnificent, methodical and persistent investigations in this regard were made by M. and Mme. Curie." The academy decided to award the Nobel Prize for Physics jointly, to Henri Becquerel and to Marie and Pierre Curie. With this decision, Marie became the first woman to receive a Nobel Prize.

Marie found out that she and Pierre had won the prize in mid-November, when a letter from the Swedish Academy arrived. The letter congratulated them, and invited them to travel to Stockholm, Sweden, to accept the prize in person and to present a public lecture on their discoveries. Pierre, who always shunned the public spotlight and hated awards, immediately wrote back, explaining that they were unable to come to Sweden. Neither of them seemed to realize the enormous significance of winning a Nobel Prize. However, the rest of the world did.

The prizes, which had been established just two years earlier, in 1901, were just beginning to gain respect. Curie—the first woman to win the prize—immediately caught the imagination of the entire world. Although the Nobel committee had not set out to make the prizes world famous, their decision to award the prize for physics to Curie catapulted both the scientist and the Nobel Prize into immediate fame. For the first time, people realized that women could make a contribution to science, a field dominated by men. With the award, the

This illustration depicts the Curies working in their laboratory. Marie and Pierre were hounded by reporters after their Nobel prize win. Publications like this one printed story after story about the couple, some of which claimed that Marie had only a minor role in the great discoveries.

Low-Key Announcement

Although the news of Marie and Pierre's Nobel Prize made headlines in Europe, it was met with only passing interest in the United States. *The New York Times* carried a small article in the December 11, 1903 issue, which read:

> "The [Nobel] prize for physics is divided between Henri Becquerel of Norway and M. and Mme. Curie of Paris. . . . Of the other recipients of this year's Nobel prizes M. and Mme. Curie are now perhaps the best known. The discoverers of radium, it is understood, have not profited financially from the work as greatly as might have been expected, and their admirers throughout the world will be delighted to hear of this windfall for them."

name "Curie" became famous around the world. It also created a fascination with the prize and with the scientific discoveries that it recognized.

Newspapers around the world rushed to report on the remarkable French couple, Marie in particular. Reporters made much of the fact that their Nobel Prize-winning discoveries were made in a broken-down storeroom with few instruments. Some reporters downplayed Marie's role in the discoveries, suggesting that she was Pierre's assistant rather than his partner. Others insisted on painting Curie as a true example of the modern woman, able to have a family and work while still maintaining her "femininity." A few, however, understood the unique and equal partnership that Marie shared with Pierre. They realized that Marie and Pierre were equal in intelligence, in skill, and that their discoveries were a true collaboration.

Marie and Pierre were completely unprepared for the waves of fame and attention that crashed into their private world. Reporters and photographers knocked on their door at all hours. If the Curies were not at home, the journalists wrote about anything they could think of. One newspaper reporter even wrote a story about the Curies' family cat! They received requests from the United States and other countries to travel and lecture about their work. The privacy-loving Curies were horrified at the idea, even though they were offered huge sums of money. They refused all offers.

STRANGE AILMENTS

Marie and Pierre viewed their Nobel Prize as more of a torment than a blessing. The prize did include a generous cash award, which Marie used to pay bills and spend on a few luxuries. But the stress of sudden fame became a tremendous burden on the intensely private couple.

The stresses of the prize and everyday life began to take their toll on both Marie and Pierre, but especially Pierre. Marie had been frail as a child, prone to fainting and nervous attacks when she was stressed. In the years after they discovered radium, they both began noticing a decline in their health. Pierre complained of joint pain and other physical ailments. It all seemed to get worse in 1903, however. It was impossible to ignore the aches, pains, and illnesses any longer. Pierre and Marie worried a great deal about each other's health. Pierre once wrote that his wife was always tired, but that she was not exactly ill. Marie became increasingly alarmed as Pierre's unexplained pains became worse. Some days his legs trembled so badly that he had to stay in bed.

Both of them blamed their stressful, busy lives for their ill health. Their friends urged them to eat, to relax, and to spend time away from the lab.

Their friends complained that the couple needed to take a break and not think of science every second of their lives. They encouraged Pierre and Marie to take a vacation and get away from science and laboratories. Although Marie and Pierre generally ignored these pleas, they did realize that the substances they were working with might be dangerous. Both of them suffered continual burns on their fingertips and hands from handling their experiments.

Regardless of the mysterious ailments, or the stress, Curie continued her study of uranium, radium, and radioactivity. She and Pierre had no intention of letting their fame get in the way of their beloved scientific research. The exciting new world of radiation had been opened up to them, and they were determined to continue discovering everything they could about "their" radium.

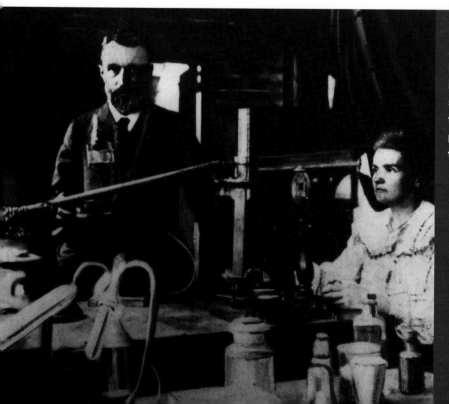

Although Marie and Pierre were frequently ill, they refused to slow down or abandon their research. This photo shows them in their lab in 1898.

SEVEN

The Dark Years

After the frantic year of 1903, when the Curies won the Nobel Prize, Marie hoped that life would return to normal. All she wanted was a chance to return to the lab, to teach her students at the Sèvres, and to raise her daughter, Irène.

At the end of the summer of 1904, Marie and Pierre received some welcome news. The Sorbonne had created a chair especially for Pierre, with the title of professor of physics of the Faculty of Sciences of the University of Paris. The job gave him a comfortable salary, but most important, the position included a fully furnished laboratory in which to work. Pierre now had a laboratory staff. Marie took the job of laboratory chief. Finally Pierre had the official French recognition that he had always deserved. Marie had a well-paying laboratory position in which she could conduct her research.

Eve Curie was born in 1904, much to the delight of Marie and Pierre. Marie had suffered a miscarriage the year before, so Eve's arrival was especially joyful to the family. Today scientists find it remarkable that both Irène and Eve were born healthy, considering Marie's long-term exposure to radiation.

Other good things came to Marie and Pierre that year. On December 6, 1904, their second daughter, Eve Denise Curie, was born. She was a chubby baby with a full head of dark hair, and Marie and Pierre adored her.

Slowly, after the frenzy of the attention from the Nobel Prize, life in the Curie household began returning to normal. Pierre's father, Eugène, had begun to help take care of the girls, which enabled Curie to spend more time in the lab. Marie and Pierre also hired a nanny, a maid, and a cook, but even with the extra help Marie sometimes felt overwhelmed. She spent every morning either at home or at school, and each afternoon in the laboratory. All of her work, plus the housekeeping, the children, the teaching, and her scientific work in the lab, left her stressed and worried. She did not know how she would manage it all, but somehow she did.

In the summer of 1905, Marie and Pierre finally made their long-postponed trip to Sweden to officially acknowledge their Nobel Prize. Pierre presented a lecture about their work to the Swedish Academy, with Marie watching proudly. Pierre was very careful to give Marie full credit for her discoveries, mentioning "Madame Curie" ten times in the speech. At other times he acknowledged that "we" made observations and discoveries together as a collaboration.

At the end of the lecture, Pierre acknowledged the potential power of radioactivity. His words echoed as a prophecy when he said, "One may also imagine that in criminal hands radium might become very dangerous, and here we may ask ourselves if humanity has anything to gain by learning the secrets of nature, if it is hope enough to profit by them, or if this knowledge is not harmful. . . . I am among those who think . . . that humanity will obtain more good than evil from the new discoveries."

Little Eve

A few months after Eve was born, Marie wrote to her brother, Jozef, about her new baby. Clearly, Marie was an attentive, if somewhat spoiling mother, telling her brother that both Irène and Eve were growing well. She said that the new baby, Eve, didn't like to sleep at all. She cried loudly if Marie left her lying awake in her cradle for too long, so Marie carried her until she quieted down. Marie lovingly described how beautiful she thought Eve was, telling Jozef that the new baby had dark hair and blue eyes, very unlike Irène, who had light hair and green-brown eyes. Marie and Pierre loved both girls and were determined to give them the best lives possible.

When Marie and Pierre returned from Sweden, they began a long summer vacation in the country. In the fall Marie, Pierre, and the children returned to Paris, rested and ready for work. Pierre was still often ill, but his new position as professor gave him renewed energy. Marie continued her own research and wrote several scientific papers on her ongoing experiments with radium and polonium. For the first time in their married lives and their careers, things were going smoothly. They were extremely busy, but they had enough money to conduct the research they wanted. They had two beautiful, healthy children and a comfortable home. The world scientific community had acknowledged and rewarded their hard work. The future looked bright, indeed.

APRIL 19, 1906

The day dawned rainy and dark. After Pierre left for work, Marie took Irène out for the day. Pierre had a meeting with fellow scientists that morning, then he enjoyed a pleasant lunch with some of his colleagues. After the meal Pierre raised his umbrella against the rain and took off on foot through the Paris streets on his way to another appointment.

Traffic in the street was heavy as the rain came down. Horse-drawn carts clattered over the cobbled streets. Pedestrians hurried to and fro, clutching their umbrellas. Automobiles chugged down the streets, honking their horns. The shouts of drivers and the whinny of horses filled the air. Pierre was oblivious to the chaos.

Suddenly a man driving a fully loaded wagon saw Pierre hurrying across the street right in front of him. The startled horses reared and knocked Pierre to the ground. In a panic, the driver jerked his horses to avoid hitting Pierre as he lay on the ground, but it was too late. The wheel of the wagon rolled over Pierre's head, killing him instantly.

The crowd quickly realized that the victim was none other than the famous scientist Pierre Curie. His body was taken to his house, where a friend, Paul Appel, was given the duty of informing Marie and Eugène Curie of the terrible event. Three hours later Marie came home to the worst news of her life. Her beloved Pierre was dead.

Soon the word flew around the world of Pierre's death. Scientists mourned the brilliant, complex man. The public wept for the great scientist and the family he left behind. Curie was in numbed shock. She had lost not only her husband and her love, but her most important scientific partner and collaborator. Later she wrote, "I lost my beloved Pierre, and with him all hope and support for the rest of my life."

Deux morts tragiques

M. Pierre CURIE, le savant qui découvrit le radium, a été écrasé dans la rue et tué net par un camion.

Un terrible accident s'est produit hier, à Paris, qui a coûté la vie à l'un des savants dont la France s'honorait. M. Curie, membre de l'Institut, célèbre par sa découverte du radium, a été écrasé par un lourd camion.

M. Curie traversait la rue Dauphine, près du Pont-Neuf, à deux heures et demie, se tenant derrière un fiacre. A ce moment arrivait du Pont-Neuf un camion attelé de

M. Curie

deux chevaux et chargé d'équipements militaires, conduit par le charretier Louis Manin.

La pente étant très rapide, le charretier ne put retenir son attelage lorsqu'il aperçut le passant qui tentait de gagner le trottoir, s'étant aperçu trop tard du danger qui le menaçait. M. Curie, s'accrochant à la tête du cheval de gauche, voulut éviter le choc, mais bientôt il lâcha prise et tomba sur le sol.

Bien que le charretier Manin eût serré son frein, entraîné par la pente, le camion continua d'avancer et les roues du lourd véhicule passèrent sur la tête de l'infortuné savant.

La mort fut instantanée et c'est un cadavre, qui fut aussitôt transporté au poste de police de la Monnaie.

This newspaper report describes Pierre's tragic death on the streets of Paris. Newspapers around the world carried the news. Marie was devastated by his death. She began keeping a diary to record her grief.

LIFE WITHOUT PIERRE

Curie was finally able to return to work a month after Pierre's death. The lab no longer held the excitement for her that it once did. Even her beloved radium seemed insignificant. The house seemed dark and empty. She visited the cemetery frequently, writing of the visits and her feelings in her journal.

Finally, it was the lab and her work, along with the demands of Irène and Eve, that pulled her back into the world of the living. One journal entry, made a few weeks after the accident, says, "I work in the laboratory all my days. I am better there than anywhere else. . . .This laboratory provides me with the illusion that I am holding on to a piece of your life and the evidence of your passage."

Slowly Curie began to recover. She had the lab, she had her family, and she still had the students whom she cared so much about. There was one

Marie's Journal

A few days after Pierre's death Marie began a journal to him. She filled it with all the pent-up emotions that she dared not share with anyone else. Author Susan Quinn related many of the journal entries in her book *Marie Curie*. About the burial, for example, Marie wrote, "I put my head against the coffin and spoke to you. I told you that I loved you and that I had always loved you with all my heart. . . . Something came to me, something like a calm and an intuition that I would yet find the courage to live."

large question in her professional life: what would happen to Pierre's chair at the Sorbonne? It seemed natural to offer the position to Marie, who was just as qualified as Pierre had been. No woman, however, had ever held a chair at the Sorbonne or been named to teach at the prestigious university. A huge debate ensued, with Curie's supporters pitted against detractors who stubbornly refused to accept a woman in this position, even one of Curie's caliber. Finally the school agreed on a compromise: they would offer her the directorship of the lab and a teaching position, but they would leave the chair vacant.

After consideration, Curie accepted the offer. She wrote in her journal, "They have offered that I should take your place, my Pierre. . . . I accepted. I don't know if it is good or bad." In November of 1906 Curie purposefully strode into the lecture hall at the Sorbonne to deliver her first lecture as professor. It was a historical moment, because she became the first woman in history to teach at the Sorbonne. The audience was filled with hundreds of well-wishers, reporters, photographers, former students, eminent scientists, and celebrities who had come to witness the occasion. No one knew what she would say. Finally Curie appeared, looking pale in a simple dark dress. When the standing ovation died down, Curie began to speak. Some in the room were astonished to hear Marie pick up Pierre's lecture exactly where he had left off. Nothing would stop Curie from doing her duty to her husband and to the science she loved.

EIGHT

New Successes, New Ordeals

Curie was alone, both personally and professionally. The almost mythic collaboration with her beloved husband, Pierre, was over. Two young daughters demanded her attention, as did her responsibilities as a professor and a scientist. Marie accepted the new challenges in her life as she had faced everything else: straightforward, with no self-pity and no second thoughts.

Marie vowed to live as Pierre would have wanted her to. Although it was difficult at first, she threw herself back into the work that they both loved. Marie found the courage to continue by trying to live by Pierre's ideals. She mentioned him and his work in her own scientific papers. She even adopted his distaste for honors and awards. In 1910, France wanted to give her the Legion of Honor, but Marie refused, explaining that it was out of respect for the memory of Pierre and his dislike of awards.

DEATH AND ACCOMPLISHMENT

The most stable force in the Curie household was her father-in-law, Eugène Curie, who had cared for Irène and Eve since before their father died. In 1909 Eugène came down with a particularly bad case of pneumonia.

Marie and the Cooperative

After Pierre's death, Marie focused on educating her daughters. The year after Pierre died she organized many of her friends who had children into a cooperative in which the adults would take turns teaching the children. The adults were all eminent scientists and scholars from a variety of fields. The group of ten children were taught English, German, French, geography, history, art, mathematics, and of course, science. The cooperative school lasted for about two years. Finally, most of the teachers became too busy with their professional lives to continue teaching the children, so the school ended. It left a lasting impression on the students. It especially affected Irène, who thrived on the intensive scientific study. She would eventually grow up to become, in 1935, the second Nobel Prize-winning woman in science (chemistry), after her mother.

He was sick for months, and the whole family was concerned. Irène was constantly by his side, upset and worried about her beloved "Grandpère." After a yearlong illness, Eugène Curie died. Marie was saddened by the loss, but Irène was devastated. She saw her grandfather's body after he had died, and she attended the funeral. For an entire year afterward she cried a great deal and worried about losing her mother as she had lost her father and grandfather. Marie did her best to comfort Irène as she coped with her own pain at the loss.

During these difficult years Curie suffered as much as her daughters did. But at the same she was also maturing into a stronger person. Slowly she was transforming from one-half of a brilliant scientific team to an esteemed scientist and person in her own right. She was growing from a celebrity into a well-respected member of the scientific world. She was taking more leadership roles in

Pierre's father, Eugène Curie, was devoted to Marie and the girls. Here, Irène snuggles on her grandpère's lap in a photo taken in 1903.

the international scientific community. Reluctantly, the world's scientists began recognizing her brilliance.

Curie wanted to prove conclusively that polonium was an element in its own right, a fact that had been disputed within the scientific community since she and Pierre had announced its existence. She began the long, arduous process of extracting polonium from pitchblende, as she had done with radium, and eventually succeeded in isolating the element. She wrote insightful scientific papers defending her work, which brought her grudging respect from even her most vocal detractors. During this period Curie was asked to prepare the International Standard for radium, a great honor. The standard measurement unit of radium would eventually be called a "curie," in her and Pierre's honor.

Women Scientists in the 1800s

Many women made significant contributions to science in the 1800s, despite the serious lack of general educational opportunities for them. Some notable Americans included Maria Mitchell, who discovered a comet in 1847. Her work in astronomy led her to become one of the first female university professors at the prestigious Vassar College. In 1886, Winifred Edgerton became the first woman to earn a Ph.D. in mathematics from Columbia University and went on to help establish Barnard College. Ellen Swallow Richards, a chemist, was one of the first scientists to study the environment and has been called "the woman who founded ecology."

After Pierre's death Marie forced herself to return to the lab. Eventually she found working to be a comfort and distraction from her grief. Her hard work and refusal to accept defeat gained her much respect among her scientific colleagues.

The scientific world had begun accepting Curie, a woman, as a brilliant scientist. She began receiving scientific honors in her own right from around the world. Curie traveled more, appearing at scientific conferences and universities around Europe to accept honorary degrees and to lecture about her work. The American millionaire Andrew Carnegie met Curie

Marie was usually the only woman at scientific conferences, such as this one in 1911. Pictured here are some of the greatest scientific minds of the time, including Marie (at the table, second from right) a young Albert Einstein (standing, second from right). Paul Langevin (far right) and Marie's romantic relationship would almost destroy Marie's scientific reputation.

and was deeply impressed by her achievements. He also respected her for being a strong woman in the scientific field. He offered to create a foundation for her, called the Curie Foundation, that would award scholarships and fund further scientific research.

Curie was pleased by the attention, but it did not detract from her main focus: her scientific work. In the years after Pierre's death she had driven herself harder, pushing herself even more deeply into her beloved science. This garnered the respect of many scientists, but it irritated others, who were never completely comfortable with a woman in their ranks.

THE SCANDAL

Paul Langevin was a respected French scientist and a good friend of the Curies for many years. He had participated in the teaching cooperative with other parents. Their families vacationed together, and their children played with one another. He had consoled Marie, along with her other close friends, when Pierre died. In the years after Pierre's death, Paul often talked to Marie about his unhappy marriage. Slowly, the two lonely, brilliant scientists forged an emotional bond that Marie came to rely on. By 1910, Marie and Paul had begun a secret affair.

Marie and Paul made every attempt to keep the affair quiet, but it could not be kept a secret for long. Eventually, Paul's wife, Jeanne, found out and, in 1911, loudly publicized the affair. The public was shocked that Curie, a brilliant scientist and grieving widow, would have a relationship with a married man. Newspapers throughout France seized on the scandal and published story after blistering story. The news gave her enemies a chance to further discredit and humiliate her.

The scandal rocked France. For the second time in a few years, Curie's intensely private world fell apart. Once again she was hounded by reporters and photographers, but this time there was a darker intent to their prying questions. Scientists who had once supported Curie now rejected her because of the scandal. Others continued to support her regardless of what the newspapers said.

Despite the public attention to her private life, Curie continued to hold her head high. She refused to allow public opinion to determine how she

Einstein Gives Marie Support

A few years before the scandal broke, Curie and the great scientist Albert Einstein had struck up a professional friendship. Over the years it had deepened, based on mutual respect and appreciation. Einstein was impressed by Marie's refusal to benefit personally from her scientific discoveries, once writing that "Marie Curie is of all celebrated beings, the one whom fame has not corrupted." He became very upset as the scandal grew larger, and he decided to write her a supportive letter. At the time, few of Marie's fellow scientists dared to support her, but Einstein had no such fears. Their friendship was more important to him than the public's opinion. In the letter, Einstein told her how much he admired her spirit, her energy, and her honesty. He told her that he considered himself fortunate to know her, and that he would always be grateful that there were people like her in the world. The words certainly comforted Marie during this dark time, and she never forgot Einstein's gesture of friendship and comfort.

would continue her life. Although she and Paul ended their intimate relationship, they remained friends for the rest of their lives. Her strength in the face
of such embarrassment and public humiliation earned her widespread respect.

A SECOND NOBEL PRIZE

Right in the middle of the great scandal Curie got some astounding and
unexpected news. For the second time, the Swedish Academy recognized
her work and awarded her the Nobel Prize. Instead of being in physics
again, this prize was in chemistry. As the Nobel citation for 1911 stated, the
prize was given "for her services in the advancement of chemistry by the
discovery of the elements radium and polonium, by the isolation of radium
and the study of the nature and compounds of this remarkable element."

Not only was she the only woman to receive the prestigious award, she
was the first person ever to be awarded two prizes. Because of the scandal
however, the French newspapers virtually ignored this historical achievement. Marie refused to let this huge personal crisis affect her scientific life.

Some members of the Swedish Academy, however, were nervous about
the escalating Langevin scandal. One member wrote her suggesting that she
decline the invitation to accept the award in person in Stockholm. Curie
wrote a polite but firm letter in response, insisting that she would indeed
attend the ceremony, pointing out that there was no connection between
her private life and her scientific accomplishments.

Curie was determined to face this challenge as she faced them all—
with dignity and strength. She traveled to Stockholm for the Nobel Prize
ceremony and gave a lecture on her work to the assembled scientists and

dignitaries. During the speech she credited Pierre with the work he had done, but she made it clear that much of the work was hers alone. Once again, Curie proved herself to the world scientific community.

The trip was a triumph for Curie, but it came at a price. The entire terrible year, culminating with the stress of the scandal and the Nobel Prize, had devastated Curie physically. When she returned from Sweden, she collapsed. By the end of 1911, Marie was diagnosed with a serious internal infection, and the doctors eventually operated on her. The operation was a success, but it left Marie even weaker and more depressed than she had been before.

For the next year she traveled to a succession of country houses and therapeutic areas in Europe and England in hopes of escaping the scandal and of curing her ailments. She was so afraid of being discovered by reporters that she used false names wherever she went. For almost the entire year of 1912, Curie was away from France. Finally, she grew stronger. The flurry of the scandal died down. Curie felt well enough to return to Paris to continue her life and her work.

THE RADIUM INSTITUTE

When Curie went back to work at her lab at the Sorbonne in late 1912, much had changed. The cost of maintaining scientific study had increased. She constantly complained about the lack of funds provided by the Sorbonne for her work. A few years before, the world-famous Pasteur Institute in France had offered to build Marie her own research facility, and now Marie seriously considered the offer. Suddenly officials at the Sorbonne were fearful that they would lose the famous Curie. They joined forces with the Pasteur Institute to create a new center devoted exclusively to the study of radioactivity. It was to be called the Radium Institute, and it would be located on a newly renamed street, the Rue Pierre Curie. Curie would run it.

By 1914, the construction of the Radium Institute was complete. Curie had been involved with almost every decision, determined that the institute would meet her exacting standards for a state-of-the-art scientific facility. That summer Curie vacationed in the country with friends. On a beautiful late summer afternoon Curie and her family got terrible news. Her work with the Radium Institute would have to wait. World War I had begun.

NINE

World War I and the Later Years

War. The thought of it filled Marie with fear. Fear for Poland and for France. Each day brought more horrible news. The Germans were advancing. They had invaded her beloved Poland; nothing was safe from the looting and burning. The world had turned upside down in a matter of weeks.

Curie decided early on that she would make some kind of contribution to the war effort to help France and her beloved Poland.

"PETITES CURIES"

It didn't take Curie long to think of a way that she could contribute to the war effort. At the time, X rays were rarely used in medicine. Curie saw the potential for X rays as a tool for doctors, so with her usual single-mindedness, she set up radiology units in hospitals and medical facilities throughout Paris. She used any equipment she could find, especially machines and other materials that were sitting unused in labs and doctors' offices that had

A few of Marie's "petite Curies" still exist. This one was displayed in Paris in 1998 to commemorate the 100th anniversary of radium.

been closed due to the war. She quickly learned to take and read simple X rays, then taught others how to do it. Curie realized that mobile radiology units were needed that could travel to where the need was greatest. She decided to create mobile radiology cars.

Curie equipped a donated automobile with machinery, equipment, and all the materials needed to take X rays. Realizing that electricity might not always be available, she even installed an electric generator in the car.

Soon there were a fleet of radiology cars. The cars that traveled wherever they were needed during the war. French soldiers fondly referred to them as "petites Curies," or "little Curies," and they became a common sight wherever wounded soldiers needed help. There were problems, however. Many doctors did not understand X rays and refused to use them. Others resented a woman telling them what to do.

Curie's Ideas Save Lives

Curie's radiology cars were only a part of her wartime effort to use science to save lives. She established field X-ray stations where wounded soldiers could be diagnosed and treated on the spot—a first for military medicine. When she realized that few medical professionals knew how to take and read X rays, Curie drove to the front and gave instructions herself. At the time, her daughter, Irène, was an intelligent and capable seventeen-year-old, and the two Curies trained personnel and assisted in taking X rays of the wounded. Eventually Irène directed X-ray facilities on her own. For three years of the war, from 1916 to 1918, Marie and Irène Curie trained more than 150 X-ray technicians at the Radium Institute in electricity, X rays, and anatomy.

Government officials decided that there was no need of the cars in the battle areas.

Once again Curie proved tougher than anyone had realized. She asked permission to take her radiology cars closer to the front lines. When she was rejected or ignored, she redoubled her efforts. Every obstacle was a challenge, and she fought with her usual vigor. When she felt that she was right, Curie was unstoppable.

Slowly her efforts paid off. With help from donations and support from various organizations, Curie bought and equipped eighteen cars. She

Marie understood the potential medical uses for X rays and took it upon herself to equip special cars with X-ray equipment. Because few people knew how to use the machinery, Marie sometimes drove the cars to the front lines herself.

personally traveled with the cars, setting up the equipment and teaching medical personnel how to work it.

Curie's contribution to the war effort transformed medical practice at the time. Doctors finally realized how effective X rays were in diagnosing and treating injuries, especially gunshot wounds. By the end of World War I, thousands of soldiers had been saved because of Curie's simple idea.

On November 11, 1918, the Germans surrendered and the Great War was over. Now, Curie could return to the lab full-time and to building the Radium Institute into the world-class facility that she and Pierre had always dreamed of.

NO MONEY TO WORK

The world after the war was a vastly different place than it had been before. Government funds were gone. Generous and wealthy patrons were dead, or their money had been depleted by the war. Curie found herself with a new facility and no means to sustain it. She would have to find financial backing for her work.

Ever since her Nobel Prize wins, Curie had been overwhelmed with requests for speaking engagements, public appearances, and invitations to hundreds of functions and parties. For the most part, Curie declined or ignored them all. Her childhood fear of speaking in public still haunted her, and even her lectures as a professor filled her with dread every time. After the Langevin scandal, she rarely agreed to interviews to the press.

It was unusual, then, that she agreed to speak to an American reporter, Marie "Missy" Meloney, the editor of an American women's magazine called the *Delineator*. One morning in May of 1920, Meloney was escorted into Curie's lab. The stylish, brash American was totally unprepared when Curie came into the room. She had expected a larger-than-life scientist, but instead she saw a small, timid woman in a simple black cotton dress and with a sad expression. Once they began talking, however, Meloney was struck by Curie's intelligence and her straightforward attitude. The meeting was the beginning of a long friendship between the two strong-willed women.

Meloney discovered that Curie's new lab was underfunded and lacked equipment. She also found out that while other countries in the world owned many grams of Curie's precious radium, France had almost none. Meloney was shocked to realize that Marie, the discoverer of radium, could not even afford to buy some for her own work.

Almost immediately Meloney came up with a bold plan. The United States would raise enough money to buy 1 gram (0.035 ounce) of radium

After Marie's disastrous experiences with reporters, she was not happy about meeting American reporter Marie Meloney (right) in 1920. However, they forged a strong friendship that lasted until Marie's death.

for Curie. At the time, 1 gram cost about $100,000. Back in the United States, Meloney used her magazine to appeal to American women to donate money to this worthy cause. By January 1921 she had raised the entire $100,000. Curie had agreed to come to the United States to accept the radium if Meloney was successful. In the spring of 1921 Curie began to plan her first trip to the United States.

MARIE IN THE UNITED STATES

Huge crowds greeted Marie, Irène, and Eve Curie as they docked in New York City in May of 1921. Hundreds of schoolchildren stretched for a glimpse of the famous Polish scientist, crowds of women from various Polish organizations in the United States waved roses in the air, and Polish flags fluttered above the crowd.

For the next few weeks, the Curie family was surrounded by hundreds of well-wishers. Marie, Eve, and

Irène (left) and Eve (center) accompanied Marie (right) on Marie's first American tour. Although Marie became sick and exhausted from the travel, Irène and Eve delighted in the crowds and the affection from the American people.

Marie received a gram of radium from President Warren G. Harding (right) during her tour of the United States. Marie's visit resulted in thousands of dollars in donations and expensive equipment for the Radium Institute.

Irène were astonished at the waves of affection that greeted them everywhere they went. All the excitement quickly exhausted Curie, although she continued to smile through the endless dinners, luncheons, appearances, and other functions. She shook so many hands that she injured her wrist and had to put it into a sling for part of her visit.

The highlight of the trip came when Curie traveled to Washington, D.C., to accept the gram of radium from President Warren G. Harding. Thousands of people came to see the historic event. Marie appeared before the huge crowd dressed in an elegant black gown, the same one she had worn at both Nobel Prize ceremonies. She smiled broadly as President Harding presented her with a small vial of radium.

Curie gave an acceptance speech, graciously saying, "I cannot express to you the emotion which fills my heart in this moment. You . . . honor me as no woman has ever been honored in America before. The destiny of a nation whose women can do what your countrywomen do today through you, Mr. President, is sure and safe. It gives me confidence in the destiny of democracy."

The trip was beginning to take its toll on Curie's fragile health. As they traveled west, Maloney agreed to cancel some scheduled engagements to preserve Curie's health. As a result, the second part of the tour was much more relaxing for Curie and her daughters. Curie came away from the trip with a new sense of the beauty of the United States and its unlimited possibilities for the future of science.

THE LATER YEARS

After the American tour, Curie was ready to finish equipping the Radium Institute and to begin its work in radioactivity. She reviewed all the applications for researchers herself and accepted a large number of women scientists. By this time she was in her fifties, becoming increasingly ill and tired, and slowly losing her eyesight to cataracts, but she was still the formidable Marie.

Irène became a well-known scientist in her own right. She worked with her famous mother, then went on to win the Nobel prize for Chemistry in 1935.

As the 1920s unfolded, the Radium Institute grew. Due to Curie's name and reputation, the lab received money grants and awards from organizations around the world. The money was used to build more labs, to buy the most up-to-date instruments and equipment, and to attract the brightest scientific minds for research and study. As a result, many major scientific discoveries about the secrets of radium were made at the institute. This brought yet more respect, fame, and funds.

DANGEROUS RAYS

By this time, the dangers of radioactivity were becoming more widely recognized. After more than twenty years of research and study, it was impossible not to notice the illnesses, weaknesses, and strange burns that plagued scientists who worked with radium.

Radiation Sickness

When Curie first isolated radium, she had no idea that the "rays" it gave off were deadly to living creatures. Radiation causes individual atoms within cells to become electrically charged, which can be very damaging. When certain cells become damaged, various sicknesses occur. For example, damage to intestinal cells can cause nausea, vomiting, and dehydration. Other symptoms of radiation poisoning include headaches, hair loss, dry cough, burning sensation, permanent skin darkening, and bleeding spots under the skin. Sometimes long-term illnesses, such as cancer or leukemia, can be caused by radiation poisoning.

Curie was now fully aware of the potentially dangerous effects of radiation. She still carried scars from burns on her fingers from decades of handling radium. Many times she wrote warnings against prolonged exposure to X rays and radiation.

The only solution was to retire, which she refused to do. Instead, she continued to attend conferences, work in the lab, and spend long months in the countryside that she loved. She wrote a biography of Pierre, and she had planned to build a house in Sceaux, the town where she had known such happiness in the past.

One of the last conferences Marie attended was the Solvay Physics conference in 1933. Attendees included Marie, her daughter Irène, Ernest Rutherford, and Paul Langevin.

By May of 1934, her health finally got the best of her. One day she worked in the lab until afternoon, then complained of a fever and went home. It was the last time she would be in her laboratory. She took to her bed, weak and sick. The doctors recommended time in a sanatorium in Switzerland, so Curie and her daughter Eve traveled there in search of a cure. By the time they reached the sanatorium, Curie was more frail and weak than she had ever been. The doctors diagnosed her with pernicious anemia, most likely the result of radiation exposure.

Curie spent her last days in bed, looking at the breathtaking views of the Swiss mountains from her window. She knew that she was dying, but she refused to be a victim to depression or regret. Ever the scientist, she insisted on reading her own temperature, even though her hands shook as she held the thermometer. Finally, on the morning of July 4, 1934, Marie Curie died. She was buried in Sceaux, beside her beloved Pierre in the French countryside that they both loved so much.

More than sixty years later, in 1995, Marie and Pierre were reburied in France's national mausoleum, the Panthéon. Many of France's most important men had been interred there. It was the final "first" for Curie. She became the first woman to be buried in this national landmark because of her own accomplishments. At the ceremony, President François Mitterand of France said, "By transferring these ashes of Pierre and Marie Curie into the sanctuary of our collective memory, France not only performs an act of recognition, it also affirms a faith in science, in research, and its respect for those who dedicate themselves to science, just as Pierre and Marie Curie dedicated their energies and their lives to science."

Timeline

1867 Maria Sklodowski is born in Warsaw, Poland, on November 7.

1873 Europe experiences an economic crisis.

1878 Maria's mother, Bronislawa, dies of tuberculosis on May 9.

1879 Thomas Edison invents the electric light.

1891 Maria begins classes at the Sorbonne in November.
She changes her name to Marie.

1893 Marie graduates from the Sorbonne with a degree in physics.

1894 Marie Sklodowski meets Pierre Curie.
Marie receives a degree in mathematics in June.

1895 Marie marries Pierre on July 26.

Wilhelm Roentgen discovers X rays.

1897 Irène Curie is born on September 12.

1898 Marie discovers polonium on February 17. Pierre and Marie announce the
discovery of radium on December 26.

1901 The first Nobel Prizes are awarded.

1903 Marie defends her thesis and becomes the first woman to earn a Ph.D. in France in June. Marie and Pierre are awarded the Nobel Prize for Physics jointly with Antoine Henri Becquerel in November.

1904 Eve Denise Curie is born on December 6.

1905 Albert Einstein publishes papers on his special theory of relativity.

1906 Pierre Curie is killed in a street accident on April 19.

1911 Marie is awarded her second Nobel Prize.

1912 The *Titanic*, a British passenger ship, sinks in the North Atlantic Ocean.

1914 The Radium Institute is complete. Marie equips the first radiology cars.

World War I begins.

1917 The Bolshevik Revolution brings Communism to Russia.

1918 World War I ends on November 11. Poland is declared an independent republic.

1921 Marie receives a gram of radium from the United States.

1929 Worldwide economic depression begins.

1934 Marie Curie dies on July 4.

To Find Out More

BOOKS

Birch, Beverly, and Christian Birmingham. *Marie Curie's Search for Radium*. New York: Barrons Juveniles, 1996.

Burby, Liza. *Marie Curie: Nobel Prize-Winning Physicist*. New York: Powerkids Press, 1997.

Pasachoff, Naomi. *Marie Curie: And the Science of Radioactivity*. New York: Oxford University Press Childrens Books, 1997.

Strathern, Paul. *Curie and Radioactivity*. New York: Anchor Books, 1999.

ORGANIZATIONS AND ONLINE SITES

Caltech Photo Archives
http://www.search.caltech.edu/Archives/action.lasso

The archive includes images of Marie Curie, taken at various times in her scientific career.

The Curie Institute
http://www.curie.fr/

This is the official Web site for the institute. It includes the names and contact information for the current directors of Marie's institute.

Distinguished Women of Past and Present
http://www.distinguishedwomen.com/index.html

This lively site includes short biographies of famous women throughout history.

Marie Curie and the Science of Radioactivity
http://www.aip.org/history/curie/contents.htm

This site, sponsored by the American Institute of Physics, includes a detailed and lively biography of Marie Curie's career.

Nobel Prize Foundation
http://www.nobel.se/physics/laureates/1903/

Included on this site is an excellent biography of Marie, with a focus on the scientific work that led to her unprecedented two Nobel Prizes.

Science in Poland: Marie Curie
http://hum.amu.edu.pl/~zbzw/ph/sci/msc.htm

This detailed site includes many entertaining facts and unusual information about Marie's life. Also included is a large list of Internet links useful to students and researchers.

A Note on Sources

Although dozens of books have been written about Marie Curie, most of them are based on a handful of excellent biographies and scientific articles. Until recently, most of Marie's private papers and journals were not available to journalists. Some of the research in this book comes from four exhaustive biographies of Marie, all of which give slightly different perspectives of her life and work. The most thorough is *Marie Curie* by Susan Quinn. Quinn was the first author to gain access to Marie's private writings and her book includes many heretofore unknown details of Marie's life. Other useful biographies included *Madame Curie*, by her daughter Eve who wrote the book only a few years after her mother's death; Rosalynd Pflaum's book, *Grand Obsession: Madame Curie and Her World*; and *Marie Curie* by Robert Reid.

A number of general biographical and scientific works were consulted, including *Uneasy Careers and Intimate Lives: Women in Science, 1789–1979*, edited by Abir-Am, Pnina, and Outram, Dorinda; *French Science and Its Principal Discoveries since the Seventeenth Century* by Maurice Caullery (New York, Arno Press, 1975); *Women of Science* edited by Kass-Simon, G., and

Farnes, Patricia, and *Scientists in Power* by Spencer R. Weart. Finally, there were a few well-researched Web sites that contained additional information, including the American Institute of Physics's exhibit titled "Marie Curie and the Science of Radioactivity" and the Nobel Prize foundation Web site containing a solid biography of Marie and Pierre's work with radioactivity.

—Allison Lassieur

Index

About the Author

Allison Lassieur has written more than forty books about famous figures, history, world cultures, current events, science, and health. In addition to writing, Ms. Lassieur studies medieval textile history. She lives in Pennsylvania.